GOVERNMENT & DEMOCRACY

by

Charlie Ogden

Crabtree Publishing Company
www.crabtreebooks.com
1-800-387-7650

Published in Canada
Crabtree Publishing
616 Welland Avenue
St. Catharines, ON
L2M 5V6

Published in the United States
Crabtree Publishing
PMB 59051
350 Fifth Ave, 59th Floor
New York, NY 10118

Published by Crabtree Publishing Company in 2017

First Published by Book Life in 2016
Copyright © 2017 Book Life

Author
Charlie Ogden

Editors
Grace Jones
Janine Deschenes

Design
Drue Rintoul

Proofreader
Crystal Sikkens

**Production coordinator and
prepress technician (interior)**
Margaret Amy Salter

Prepress technician (covers)
Ken Wright

Print coordinator
Katherine Berti

Printed in Hong Kong/012017/BK20161024

Photographs

Keystone Press: © Christopher Pike/ ZUMAPRESS.com:
   page 13
Shutterstock: Angelo Giampiccolo: page 5; FashionStock.com:
   page 8; Alexey Stiop: page 9 (top); Drop of Light: page 10;
   Osugi: page 11; Art Babych: page 12; Everett Collection:
   page 14; Viktoria Gaman: page 17; Slavko Sereda: page 23;
   Everett Historical: page 24; Featureflash Photo Agency:
   page 25; knyazevfoto: page 29
Thinkstock Photos: front cover (top)
   Wikimedia Commons: AlMare: front cover (bottom)
Other images by Shutterstock

Front cover:
   (top) Palace of Westminster in London, England, where the
   British Houses of Parliament meet
   (bottom); Former president, Barack Obama, the first African
   American president of the United States

Library and Archives Canada Cataloguing in Publication

Ogden, Charlie, author
   Government and democracy / Charlie Ogden.

(Our values)
Issued in print and electronic formats.
ISBN 978-0-7787-3266-2 (hardback).--ISBN 978-0-7787-3349-2
(paperback).--ISBN 978-1-4271-1897-4 (html)

   1. Political science--Juvenile literature. 2. Democracy--
Juvenile literature. I. Title.

JA70 O43 2016   j320   C2016-906665-7
                                     C2016-906666-5

Library of Congress Cataloging-in-Publication Data

CIP available at Library of Congress

CONTENTS

Words in **bold** can be found in the glossary on page 31.

WHAT IS A GOVERNMENT?

A government is a system that regulates a certain area, such as a country. It is made up of a group of people that provide rules, **authority**, and order for everyone living in the area. Today, every country in the world has a government. For many countries this is a good thing, as a government is able to organize the people and **resources** in a way that is best for its **citizens**. However, while governments are supposed to do all they can to help the people in their countries, some governments are more effective at doing this than others.

WE CALL DEBATES AND QUESTIONS ABOUT HOW GOVERNMENTS SHOULD WORK "POLITICS."

The Grand Kremlin Palace in Moscow, Russia, is the place where the Russian government conducts its business.

In order for the people in a government to be able to help and protect the citizens in their country, they need to be able to do a lot of things. They need to have the power to stop people from doing harmful things, be able to help people who are in trouble, and have the resources to build **facilities** for different communities, amongst many other things.

For a government to achieve all of this, it needs a lot of money. One way that governments often raise this money is through tax. They use the money from taxes to buy large and often expensive buildings for the people in their countries to use, such as schools and hospitals. Governments also use taxes to pay the **salaries** of government workers, such as police officers.

This is a police officer in India. He is paid for the work he does from money collected through taxes.

WHAT IS TAX?

Tax is the money that the people in a country pay to their government so that the government can do things such as offer health care to people and build schools, roads, and hospitals. Taxes are often added on to the things people buy, or taken from the money they earn.

WHY IS A GOVERNMENT IMPORTANT?

Philosopher Thomas Hobbes wrote about what life might be like for people without a government. He said that if there was no government, people would be more likely to commit crimes, such as harming or stealing from others, because there would be no laws or police officers to stop them. Governments help to provide protection and safety to the people that they govern. They help **communities** of people live and work together peacefully. Governments also make sure that people have the services they need to survive and succeed, such as school and health care. They make communities better places to live. Governments control a number of things that we depend on every day, such as money, laws, and assistance.

Thomas Hobbes

MONEY

We rely on money every day in order to buy the things we need to survive, such as food, and the things we want. Governments control the supply, or amount, of money that is available in a country. Usually they do this using **central banks**, a government institution that manages money. Through central banks, governments can print money when it is needed.

Governments are needed to regulate money so that the money supply is consistent, allowing people access to the money they need to buy things. When people are able to buy things, this helps the **economy** because businesses make money. Although some people disagree on how much a government should regulate money, it is important for a government to try to make sure that money is available to help keep people, businesses, and the economy afloat.

DISASTER AID

Natural disasters, such as floods and earthquakes, may leave people homeless without food or water and in great danger. When this happens, governments often have money set aside in order to provide **aid** on a large scale. For example, during floods, governments may send rescuers in boats to help people that are trapped due to flood waters. They may also parachute-in food supplies from airplanes, and work to reduce the level of the flood waters— and this can all be done at the same time!

If the disaster is particularly bad, a government can also organize fund-raising plans to help the people affected by the disaster, or ask governments from other countries for additional help. Government help is also crucial in rebuilding an area after a disaster. For example, the Canadian government has given over 300 million dollars to help rebuild Fort McMurray, Alberta, after a wildfire destroyed most of the city.

The United States army was sent to provide assistance to those affected by Hurricane Sandy in 2012. Here, they pass out supplies, such as water bottles, in New York for people who lost their homes and belongings.

LAWS

One of the most important things a government can do for a country is create and enforce laws that benefit its citizens. Laws are rules made by the government that everyone in a country must follow. A country's laws are meant to protect the people that are living there. People who do not follow the law are committing a crime, which they can be punished for. As punishment, a person may be sent to prison, have to pay a fine, or work within the community for free.

A government is chosen to represent the voices and needs of the people in a country. Therefore, the government needs to create laws that take its citizens' needs into consideration. Sometimes the opinions of the public, as well as pressure from the media, can push a government to pass a law. In many countries, there are organizations known as pressure or interest groups that work to influence laws and public policies.

Fox hunting was banned in the U.K. in 2004 due to pressure from the public and the media.

The Ukrainian flag

Governments have the job of creating new laws that are fair for everyone. Some laws are easy to make because almost everyone agrees with them. Others can involve a lot of complicated factors that not everyone agrees with, such as the laws that determine the amount of taxes people should pay. Governments are best at deciding on the laws because they have the money and information to figure out the best way to meet the needs of all people.

Governments are also made up of a lot of people from different backgrounds that can give different perspectives and make sure the laws are appropriate for all types of people. Often, governments even have to work together with governments from other countries to create international laws and agreements that benefit everyone.

INTERNATIONAL LAWS

Usually, a government makes its own laws that decide how a country is run. However, there are also international laws that governments in many countries must follow. International laws are made by the United Nations, which is a partnership of 193 countries that work together to solve world issues. The United Nations General Assembly, made up of representatives from each country, proposes and votes on international laws using a **democratic process**. When a law, or treaty, is decided, UN member countries decide whether to sign the treaty and follow the law. Such treaties include laws on the rights of children and people with disabilities.

International laws that are followed by the members of the United Nations cover a wide range of issues, including the way countries act during war, human rights, and refugees. UN member countries must follow the international laws that regulate spaces that are not owned by any one government, such as outer space, international waters, and the environment.

The headquarters for the United Nations are in New York City. The flags of each of the member nations are displayed.

MEMBERS OF GOVERNMENT

Governments are organized in many different ways, some of which are very complicated. However, most governments will have a single person who is considered to be the head of that government. This person is usually called a prime minister or president.

Justin Trudeau is Canada's prime minister. He was elected in 2015.

Executive Branch

In the United States, the head of the government is called the president. There is also a vice president who assists the president. Many governments also contain groups of people known as cabinets. Cabinets advise heads of government on current issues and decide how the country should be run. The United States government has a cabinet of 15 members. In Canada and the United Kingdom, the head of government is called the prime minister. The prime minister is supported by his or her cabinet. In Canada, the cabinet has 30 members, each of whom are called ministers. The United Kingdom's cabinet has 21 members. The head of government and the cabinet make up the executive branch of **parliament**, or an **elected** body of government.

Parliament

There are two branches of Parliament, or government, in Canada and the United Kingdom. The executive branch makes decisions on how to run the country, while the legislative branch of government makes the laws. Some laws may be proposed by a member of the cabinet, but the legislative branch decides whether the laws should be passed, or made official. In Canada, the legislative branch is made up of two houses: the Senate and the House of Commons. A bill, or proposed law, is first introduced in the House of Commons. When the House of Commons agrees, it is sent to the Senate. If the Senate agrees, the bill can become a law.

Canada was originally part of the United Kingdom and run by the king or queen of Britain. Today, the British king or queen no longer runs the country, but is still a part of Canada's Parliament. The governor general represents the king or queen in Canada. David Johnston is Canada's current governor general.

CANADIAN LEGISLATIVE BRANCH

HOUSE OF COMMONS
Made up of members of parliament (MPs) who have been elected by the public. There are 338 members in the House of Commons.

SENATE
Made up of people chosen by the prime minister. There are 105 seats in the Senate.

United States GOVERNMENT

The executive branch is only one part of the United States government. When the United States of America first became a country, a document was written that explained how the government should be set up and how the country should be run. This document is called the United States Constitution and it explains that the US government should have three parts so that no individual person or group can ever have too much power. The legislative branch of the United States government is called Congress. It includes the Senate, and the House of Representatives.

Barack Obama, the 44th president of the United States

THE PRESIDENT

The president is the most important person in the United States government. The president has to agree that the new laws and policies suggested by Congress are going to benefit the American people. He or she is able to veto, or stop, any law that is passed by Congress. It is the president's job to decide the most effective way to put them into action.

CONGRESS

The role of Congress in the United States government is very similar to that of the Senate and House of Commons in the Canadian government. They are a group of people who are responsible for suggesting, amending, and deciding new laws and policies for the country.

US CONGRESS
NUMBER OF PEOPLE:
535

SENATE
NUMBER OF PEOPLE:
100

Two people are elected as senators for each of the 50 states. Senators create and vote on laws.

HOUSE OF REPRESENTATIVES
NUMBER OF PEOPLE:
435

Representatives, also called congressmen or congresswomen, are elected by the public.

THE SUPREME COURT

The Supreme Court is the third part of government. Its job is to make sure that none of the new laws suggested by Congress go against what is said in the United States Constitution. The Supreme Court also makes the final decision in cases where it is uncertain whether a law has been broken.

The United States Supreme Court building

15

GOVERNMENTS
AROUND THE WORLD

JAPAN

The Japanese flag

Japan formed a new government in 1947, after the **Second World War**, and wrote a constitution that explained how the country should be run. There is a specific part of the Japanese Constitution that is unlike the constitution of any other government in the world—it stops Japan from ever going to war. Japan has not fought a war against another country since the Second World War and if it follows its own constitution, it never will. Japan still has an army, but it cannot be used to attack other countries. The role of Japan's army is only to defend itself in case it is attacked by another country.

Japan

Tokyo, the capital city of Japan

NORTH KOREA

North Korea became a country in 1948 and when it did, a man named Kim Il-sung was made the president. Since then, the North Korean government has become a dictatorship where rule over the country has passed straight from father to son without a democratic election. North Korea has been a dictatorship for over 60 years.

DICTATORSHIP

A dictatorship is a form of government where one person, or sometimes a small group of people, make all of the decisions for a country.

Pyongyang, the capital city of North Korea

North Korea

The North Korean flag

Because the North Korean government is ruled by one person only, decisions often benefit the government rather than the public. The current North Korean dictator, Kim Jong-un, and many people who are close to him, seem to live expensive lifestyles in big houses, whereas much of the North Korean population struggles to find enough food to survive. However, it is difficult to be exactly sure what is going on in North Korea as it is one of the most secretive countries in the world. The government only allows very few people to enter the country, and citizens cannot freely leave.

BHUTAN

Bhutan is a very small country in Asia. However, in 1972, Bhutan introduced a policy that made **politicians** around the world change their view of what they thought made a successful government. The King of Bhutan, known as Dragon King Jigme Singye Wangchuck, declared that the happiness of the people in Bhutan should be used to measure how well the country's government was doing. In Bhutan, Gross National Happiness is the most important factor in measuring the government's success or failure.

The Bhutanese flag

The United Nations (UN) flag. The UN is an important organization that works with governments all over the world. They have, along with Bhutan, made happiness one of their main considerations when deciding how successful a government is.

Bhutan

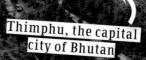

Thimphu, the capital city of Bhutan

SOMALIA

Somalia's government has been unstable for many years. In 1991, a **civil war** broke out in Somalia and the Somali government was removed from power by some of the Somali public. A new government could not be formed in Somalia for many years as the civil war and a severe **drought** used much of the country's resources, making it very difficult for any group of people to create change in the country. Since there was no government, many different groups fought for power in the country.

In 2000, a Somali government was established for the first time in nearly ten years. However, this new government was only ever in control of a very small area of Somalia, leaving most of Somalia's population to survive the civil war without help from a government.

The Somali flag

Mogadishu, the capital city of Somalia

The federal government of Somalia was finally created in 2012, after 17 attempts to create a new government. By this time, most of the country had spent over 20 years living without a government.

Somalia

WHAT IS A DEMOCRACY?

A democracy is a system of government that gives power to the people within a country—people decide how their country is run by electing members of the government to represent them. Living within a democracy means that the people in a country get to take part in the decisions made by their government. Any kind of government that is influenced by public opinion is called a democracy; however, this doesn't mean that all democracies are the same. In the past, it used to be that only men, or even just rich men, could take part in the decisions of a government. Today, a lot of countries accept that everyone should have a say in a democracy. Usually, the only condition is that you have to be above a certain age.

OFFICIAL BALLOT

BALLOT BOX

For Official Use Only

Often people vote for members of government by selecting on a secret ballot, or piece of paper, who they would like to see elected. The ballots are then placed in a ballot box or electronic scanner to be counted.

DIRECT AND REPRESENTATIVE DEMOCRACIES

There are two main types of democracy—a direct democracy and a representative democracy. A direct democracy is where the public can vote on every decision made by their government. This is often not a realistic way to run a government, especially in countries with a lot of people. Governments in big countries have to make a lot of decisions and there often isn't enough time to find out what everyone in the country wants the government to do.

People in representative democracies instead vote on who they want to govern their countries. This happens every few years through **general elections.** After the votes have been counted and a government has been chosen, the people in that country usually do not get to vote on every law or policy. Instead, their elected representatives do this on behalf of the general public. If the public feel that the government is not representing their interests, they can choose to vote for a different party or politician during the next general election.

The United States government is a representative democracy and usually has a general election every four years. The two main **political parties** in the U.S. are Democratic and Republican.

WHY IS A DEMOCRACY IMPORTANT?

Democratic governments are important because they often lead to positive outcomes for the people in those countries. In particular, democracies offer the freedom of choice for their people, and allow them to have a say in the way their countries are run. Because people feel the system is fair, democracy often leads to a **stable government**.

Some non-democratic countries don't give their citizens the freedom to choose their own religion. This is the case in Saudi Arabia, where every citizen must be Muslim by law.

Most people want the freedom to choose the way they live their lives. In most democracies the members of government encourage freedom by listening to and acting upon the views and beliefs of the people that they govern. For something to become law in a democratic government, a majority of people have to agree on it. Extreme views about things such as marriage and religion aren't often held by a majority of people. A democracy stops extreme views from being made into laws and preserves people's freedom to choose.

Democratic countries, if run properly, often have the support of many of their citizens. This is because politicians are elected by the public and usually try to represent the citizens' interests. This greatly reduces the chance of civil war as people are not likely to attack a government which they chose.

Countries that are run by a dictator, on the other hand, are more likely to break out into civil war. Dictators are usually not elected. They are leaders that hold absolute power and can do anything they want with their countries. This can lead to civil war when the citizens want to remove a dictator.

In 2011, a civil war broke out in Libya in order to overthrow the dictator Muammar Gaddafi.

WHAT ISN'T A DEMOCRACY?

DICTATORSHIP

A dictatorship is a system of government in which one person controls a country. The leader of a dictatorship, known as a dictator, can gain power in a number of ways. Sometimes, they work their way up through a democratic government and then, when they have enough power to do so, they change the government into a dictatorship and put themselves in charge. Other times, a group of people who are against the current government may start a civil war in the country. During the civil war, they will force the leader out of power and put their own dictator in charge instead.

One of the most famous dictators of all time was Adolf Hitler, who was the German dictator before and during the Second World War.

MONARCHY

Another way of governing a country is through a monarchy. Within a monarchy, one member of a royal family, called the monarch, rules over the country. While every member of the ruling family in a monarchy will have some power, only the monarch is considered to be the leader of the country. When the monarch dies, another member of the same family takes over—usually their eldest son. In many countries, the person who rules a monarchy is called a king or a queen. In other places, such as countries in Asia, they are often called an emperor or an empress.

Queen Elizabeth II is technically the ruler of the United Kingdom, but the democratic government makes almost all of the important decisions.

There are very few monarchies left in the world today. In fact, many of the monarchies that still exist don't really count as a monarchy. This is because the king, queen, emperor, or empress do not have much power over how the country is run. Instead, these countries often have a government that runs the country.

DEMOCRACY IN HISTORY

This is the Parthenon, a temple dedicated to the Ancient Greek goddess Athena. It was built during the time that Athens was a democracy, roughly 2,500 years ago.

Many people believe that the principles of democracy were founded over 2,500 years ago in the ancient city of Athens, Greece. Athens is now the capital city of Greece, however at that point in time it was an independant city that ruled itself, much like a country does today. Until this point in history, nearly all countries were controlled by a monarch or a dictator. This meant that many people in Athens at the time were interested and excited by the new idea of democracy—one in which they would have a say in how the city was controlled. Athens had a direct democracy, so the public could vote on every decision made by the government.

Although Athens used a system of government that would later be adopted by many countries around the world, there were some ways in which the democracy in Athens was flawed. The main reason was that it didn't allow everyone to vote. Only the rich men in the community could vote. Poor men, women, and slaves had no say in what the government did. However, this is not very unusual for the time. Women did not receive the right to vote in the United States until 1920, and in Canada until 1918. Even then, not all women received the right to vote—in some places, certain non-white men and women did not have the right to vote until decades later.

The Acropolis, an ancient **citadel** in Athens

Even though the democratic government in Athens wasn't perfect, it was still ahead of its time. Athens had a democratic government for less than 200 years before it was conquered and turned into a monarchy under the rule of King Philip of Macedonia. Athens returned to a democratic system around 2,000 years later.

DEMOCRACY IN THE WORLD

Many studies have been done in order to determine which countries are democratic and which are not. Since governments are so large, with many different parts, governments can have parts that are democratic and parts that are not.

Democratic

Partially democratic

Non-democratic

Most democratic governments today exist in Western Europe, North America, and South America. However, there are strong democratic governments outside of these areas, such as in Australia, Japan, South Africa, and India. Most countries in Africa and Asia are ruled by some sort of dictatorship.

Many other countries in Africa and Asia, and a few in South America, have governments that have some elements of democracy and some elements of dictatorship. This is a good sign—it shows that countries in these areas are beginning to move toward a democratic form of government.

The most democratic countries in the world, according to the **Democracy Index**, are in northern Europe. Norway, Sweden, Denmark, and other countries in the same area of Europe are believed by many to have the most stable and democratic governments in the world.

This is possibly because of the size of these countries. Many of the countries in this area of Europe are very small and have populations of fewer than 10 million people, which makes it a lot easier to maintain a strong democratic government and collect votes from everyone in the country. However, this can't be the only reason that they are democratic, as there are a lot of countries that are even smaller than these that do not have democratic governments.

A man in India's capital, New Delhi. India is the largest democratic country in the world. It collected over 800 million votes in its last election.

THINK ABOUT IT!

1 Be like Thomas Hobbes! In what ways would life change if there were no governments giving rules, order, and protection to communities?

2 Describe a time that you have been involved in a democratic decision. How do you know that it was democratic?

3 What do you think is the most important benefit of a democratic system of government? Why?

GLOSSARY

aid	Help or assistance
authority	The right or power to control, give orders, and make decisions
central banks	National institutions that manage currency, money supply, and regulation
citadel	A walled area in the center of a city
citizens	Legally recognized members of a country
civil war	A war between citizens of the same country, often fought against a government or ruling power
community	A group of people who live, work, and play in a place
constitution	A collection of rules that state how a government should work or run
Democracy Index	A list compiled by the Economist Intelligence Unit that measures democracy in 167 countries, using rankings in different categories
democratic process	A government practice that involves the public in decision making
drought	A long period of very little rainfall, leading to a lack of water
economy	A place in which goods and services are produced, distributed, bought, and sold
elected	Voted by the public to be part of government
facilities	Buildings or pieces of equipment provided for a specific purpose
general elections	Where the main parties in governments are voted for by the public
interest groups	An organization of people who hold a common interest and work together to influence the government in favor of that interest
parliament	An elected body of government that deals with laws
philosopher	A person who studies the nature of knowledge, reality, and existence
policies	Rules or courses of action adopted by organizations or governments
political party	A group of people who have similar ideas about how a government should be run
politicians	People who are professionally involved in government and politics
resources	Supplies of money, materials, or people
salaries	Payments to an employee for work
Second World War	From 1939 to 1945, a major war fought between the Allies (including Great Britain, Canada, and the United States) and the Axis Powers (including Germany, Italy, and Japan)
stable government	A government that is resistant to sudden change or collapse

INDEX